A Fresh Approach
to Sight-Reading

Joining the Dots
for Violin

Grade 1

Alan Bullard

Violin Consultant: Douglas Blew

ABRSM

To the Teacher

Joining the Dots offers lots of material to help build skill and confidence in sight-reading. Used as part of regular lessons and practice, it will help pupils learn to read new music more quickly and easily, developing their awareness of fingerboard geography, their sense of key and other general musicianship skills.

The five books in the series cover the keys found in ABRSM's sight-reading tests at each of Grades 1–5, with a section for each key. (In this Grade 1 book there are two sections for each key.) Each section begins with warm-up and technical material ('Key Features' and 'Workouts'), followed by opportunities for improvisation ('Make Music') and several short pieces to sight-read ('Read and Play').

Key Features are a supplement to scales and arpeggios, and will help pupils to establish the 'feel' of each key under the fingers. They can be played at various speeds and dynamics, and with the different bowing suggested.

Workouts are for warming up and exercising in the key. They are designed to be practised, and therefore explore slightly more advanced techniques than those found in sight-reading at this level. To help reinforce key familiarity, the Workouts are the same (transposed for each key) in the first two sections (fingers 1 & 2); those in the last two sections (fingers 1, 2 & 3) are also identical apart from key.

Make Music provides an opportunity for your pupils to build confidence in (and through) creative and imaginative work, and to develop aural skills. The activities here will also help to familiarize pupils with the 'feel' of the key, but using an approach that is not primarily notation-based. The first is always an 'echo' piece, which will help with listening skills and relate these to the fingerboard; the other two are more creative, and you and your pupils can approach these together in whatever way is most comfortable: for most pupils this will involve exploring the violin with some trial and error – experimenting is a good way to learn here!

Read and Play is the goal of each section – a number of short, characterful pieces, to be played at sight or after a short practice time, with the focus on keeping going. These lead up to and include the technical standard to be found in Grade 1 sight-reading and are a useful source of sight-reading material for those preparing for exams. The last piece in this section is usually slightly longer than the pieces found in Grade 1 sight-reading.

It is suggested that pupils use the sections for 1st and 2nd fingers before moving on to those for all three fingers. Within each section, it is recommended that pupils learn and play the Key Features and Workouts before moving on to the Make Music and Read and Play material.

Towards the end of the book you will find **More Pieces to Play**, including solo pieces, and duets and a trio suitable for group work. Some of these are longer and slightly more challenging than the pieces found in Grade 1 sight-reading. The material in this section can be used in any way you wish – as additional sight-reading practice or as pieces to learn quickly and play through for fun.

First published in 2013 by ABRSM (Publishing) Ltd, a wholly owned subsidiary of ABRSM, 24 Portland Place, London W1B 1LU, United Kingdom

© 2013 by The Associated Board of the Royal Schools of Music

AB 3708

Illustrations by Willie Ryan, www.illustrationweb.com/willieryan
Book design and cover by www.adamhaystudio.com
Music and text origination by Julia Bovee
Printed in England by Caligraving Ltd, Thetford, Norfolk

Dear Violinist,

Joining the Dots will help you to learn new music more quickly and easily.

In this book you will find sections for each key that you are likely to use in Grade 1 sight-reading.

In each section there are several different things to do:

Key Features to get you used to playing in the key

Make Music in which you can develop and explore musical ideas

Workouts to exercise your fingers and bowing arm

Read and Play where there are a number of short pieces to play – read the title, work out the rhythm, find the notes and, when you're ready, play the piece right through without stopping!

Towards the end of the book you'll find **More Pieces to Play**, including some longer pieces, and duets and a trio to play with your friends.

Enjoy Joining the Dots!

Alan Bullard

D major (fingers 1 & 2)

Key Features

- Practise these in various ways – loudly and quietly, fast and slow
- Always listen to the tuning

- Play this with separate bows throughout, or with two crotchets to a bow in bars 1–3

- Using separate bows throughout, aim for an even tone and smooth bow-changes

Workouts

- Practise these workouts to warm up in the key of D major

- Play this neatly and rhythmically

- Take care to make the tone even

Make Music

Echoing Footsteps

- Make a tune with your teacher by repeating each phrase, in time
- Your teacher will show you which note to start on and count in two bars to set the pulse
- Don't look at the music or at your teacher's fingers – just listen

Andante

(teacher) (echo) (teacher) (echo) (teacher) (echo)

mf

You can also try singing these echoes to 'la'.

My Cat

Make a tune to fit the words below:

- First of all, say the words out loud to make a rhythm
- Then turn the rhythm into a tune, using the open D and A strings and perhaps the 1st and 2nd fingers
- Start and finish on the note D

My black cat's called Daisy; she is very lazy.

You can sing along with the words while you play, if you like.

A Tune in Time

- Tap this rhythm several times
- When you can do it, make the rhythm into a tune using the D and A strings (open and fingered)
- Start and finish on the note D

Happily

f

D major (fingers 1 & 2)

Read and Play

- Look at the time signature and count two bars of crotchets, out loud
- Keep counting, and tap the rhythm
- Then check the key signature and the first note, and get your fingers and bow ready
- If you like, try out the piece first
- Finally, play it right through without stopping!

For *On the Move* and *By the Lake* there's a duet part for your teacher.

On the Move

- Keep a steady beat in this march

By the Lake

- Create a calm and peaceful mood here

• Remember to try out the rhythm first, then check the key signature and the first note

Knocking on the Door

• Count the rest carefully in bar 4

Peaceful Thoughts

• Play this steadily and gently

Cat and Mouse

• Make as much contrast as you can between the loud and quiet dynamics

Dancing Duet

• Here's a lively dance to play with a friend
• The second player plays the same music, beginning when the first player reaches the asterisk sign (✱)

A major (fingers 1 & 2)

Key Features

- Practise these in various ways – loudly and quietly, fast and slow
- Always listen to the tuning

- Play this with separate bows throughout, or with two crotchets to a bow in bars 1–3

- Using separate bows throughout, aim for an even tone and smooth bow-changes

Workouts

- Practise these workouts to warm up in the key of A major

- Play this neatly and rhythmically

- Take care to make the tone even

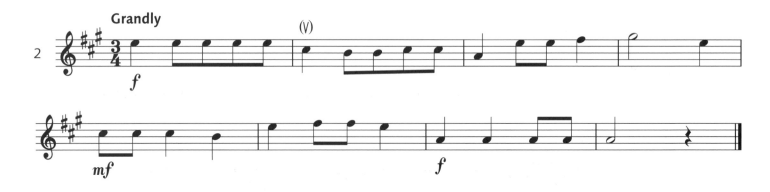

Make Music

A Major Echo

- Make a tune with your teacher by repeating each phrase, in time
- Your teacher will show you which note to start on and count in two bars to set the pulse
- Don't look at the music or at your teacher's fingers – just listen

Allegretto

(teacher) (echo) (teacher) (echo) (teacher) (echo)

You can also try singing these echoes to 'la'.

Hot-Air Balloon

Make a tune to fit the words below:

- First of all, say the words out loud to make a rhythm
- Then turn the rhythm into a tune, using the open A and E strings and perhaps the 1st and 2nd fingers
- Start and finish on the note A

Floating high above the trees, gently swaying in the breeze.

You can sing along with the words while you play, if you like.

Hopping

- Tap this rhythm several times
- When you can do it, make the rhythm into a tune using the A and E strings (open and fingered)
- Start and finish on the note A

Andante

A major (fingers 1 & 2)

Read and Play

- Look at the time signature and count two bars of crotchets, out loud
- Keep counting, and tap the rhythm
- Then check the key signature and the first note, and get your fingers and bow ready
- If you like, try out the piece first
- Finally, play it right through without stopping!

For *The End of the Day* and *Happy Holiday* there's a duet part for your teacher.

The End of the Day

- Imagine the sun setting slowly over the horizon

Happy Holiday

- Make this piece rhythmic and joyful

• Remember to try out the rhythm first, then check the key signature and the first note

Stylish Sarabande

• A sarabande is a stately dance, which originally came from Spain

Starry Night

• Create a calm mood with expressive playing

Raindrops

• Suggest the drops of rain by playing this piece as delicately and gently as you can

Walking

• Here's a piece to play with a friend
• The second player plays the same music, beginning when the first player reaches the asterisk sign (✱)

D major (fingers 1, 2 & 3)

Key Features

- Practise these in various ways – loudly and quietly, fast and slow
- Always listen to the tuning

- Play this with separate bows throughout, or with two crotchets to a bow in bars 1–3

- Using separate bows throughout, aim for an even tone and smooth bow-changes

Workouts

- Practise these workouts to warm up in the key of D major

- Play this neatly and rhythmically

- Let this piece float along smoothly, with controlled bowing

Make Music

Nearly Home!

- Make a tune with your teacher by repeating each phrase, in time
- Your teacher will show you which note to start on and count in two bars to set the pulse
- Don't look at the music or at your teacher's fingers – just listen

Allegretto

(teacher)   (echo)   (teacher)   (echo)   (teacher)   (echo)

mf

f

You can also try singing these echoes to 'la'.

Window Shopping

Make a tune to fit the words below:

- First of all, say the words out loud to make a rhythm
- Then turn the rhythm into a tune, using any notes from the D major scale
- Start and finish on the note D

Walking down the high street, looking in the shops.

You can sing along with the words while you play, if you like.

Marching By

- Tap this rhythm several times
- When you can do it, make the rhythm into a tune in the key of D major
- Start on any note of the scale but finish on the note D

Rhythmic and steady

f

D major (fingers 1, 2 & 3)

Read and Play

- Look at the time signature and count two bars of crotchets, out loud
- Keep counting, and tap the rhythm
- Then check the key signature and the first note, and get your fingers and bow ready
- If you like, try out the piece first
- Finally, play it right through without stopping!

For *By the River* and *Best Foot Forward* there's a duet part for your teacher.

By the River

- Think of a rowing boat floating smoothly down a river

Best Foot Forward

- Imagine you are marching steadily along a road

• Remember to try out the rhythm first, then check the key signature and the first note

Coming Down the Stairs

• Count carefully and don't rush!

Bouncing Ball

• Aim for a tight, 'springy' rhythm here

Question and Answer

• Make the answer louder than the question!

Two in Step

• Here's a piece to play with a friend
• The second player plays the same music, beginning when the first player reaches the asterisk sign (✱)

A major (fingers 1, 2 & 3)

Key Features

- Practise these in various ways – loudly and quietly, fast and slow
- Always listen to the tuning

- Play this with separate bows throughout, or with two crotchets to a bow in bars 1–3

- Using separate bows throughout, aim for an even tone and smooth bow-changes

Workouts

- Practise these workouts to warm up in the key of A major

- Play this neatly and rhythmically

- Let this piece float along smoothly, with controlled bowing

Make Music

Echo Waltz

- Make a tune with your teacher by repeating each phrase, in time
- Your teacher will show you which note to start on and count in two bars to set the pulse
- Don't look at the music or at your teacher's fingers – just listen

Like a waltz

You can also try singing these echoes to 'la'.

Running for the Bus

Make a tune to fit the words below:

- First of all, say the words out loud to make a rhythm
- Then turn the rhythm into a tune, using any notes from the A major scale
- Start and finish on the note A

Running, running, running fast, running for the bus.

You can sing along with the words while you play, if you like.

Happy Hamster

- Tap this rhythm several times
- When you can do it, make the rhythm into a tune in the key of A major
- Start on any note of the scale but finish on the note A

Lively

A major (fingers 1, 2 & 3)

Read and Play

- Look at the time signature and count two bars of crotchets, out loud
- Keep counting, and tap the rhythm
- Then check the key signature and the first note, and get your fingers and bow ready
- If you like, try out the piece first
- Finally, play it right through without stopping!

For *Far from Home* and *Rocking Chair* there's a duet part for your teacher.

Far from Home

- Make this melody sad and expressive

Teacher's
part
(optional)

Rocking Chair

- Imagine you are rocking backwards and forwards, slowly and gently

Teacher's
part
(optional)

18

• Remember to try out the rhythm first, then check the key signature and the first note

I'm Late!

• Play this piece as fast as you can, but don't let it run away with you – count carefully

Yachting

• Try to suggest a sailing boat drifting in the breeze

Calling Birds

• Imagine that two birds are singing to each other

Scaly Duet

• Here's a smooth and flowing piece to play with a friend
• The second player plays the same music, beginning when the first player reaches the asterisk sign (✱)

More Pieces to Play

- On the remaining pages you will find a variety of solo pieces of different lengths, and some duets and a trio to play with your friends
- You can use these for playing at sight, or as pieces to learn on your own or with your teacher
- Before you start to play, don't forget to check the key signature and time signature, make sure you can tap the rhythm, and then get your fingers and bow ready

Sunshine and Clouds

Evening Calm

Aiming High

Looking Across the Lake

Gently Dreaming

Nightfall

On the Swing

Up and Down

Folk Dance

Mighty Minuet

More Pieces to Play

I Agree!

Butterflies

Falling Leaves

Blue Sky

Passing By

Barbecue Bop

10:15